Legacy Play

The Five Elements of a Lasting, Personal Legacy

Bruce Goeas | Steve Darr

Printed in the United States of America

First Printing, July 2018

ISBN: 9781980932291

Acknowledgements

Rarely is a legacy a solo venture. *Legacy Play* is no exception.

We would like to thank:

Dana Perino, former White House Press Secretary to President George W. Bush and host of The Daily Briefing with Dana Perino on Fox News

For your insights, thoughtfulness, and civility setting an example we all could well emulate. Thank you for all you do and who you are.

Ervin Rokke, Lt. General, USAF, Retired; former President Moravian College, former President of National Defense University

For leading by example and the legacies represented in those you have taught and led. Thank you for your support and guidance. Thank you for always leaving the woodpile higher when you departed.

Blake Fennell, President & CEO, Abrisa Technologies

For proving that grace and humility are essential ingredients in being a leader. Thank you for your inputs and support.

Ed Goeas, President & CEO, Tarrance Group

For being my hero from day one. I have benefited a great deal from your advice and mentorship through the years. Thank You.

Contents

INTRODUCTION

It is January 17, 2127, and two college students, Henrik and Alesha, are sipping coffee. Their Humanities professor at the University of Stockholm has challenged the class to identify one, and only one, trait for a seemingly incongruous, diverse set of 19th, 20th, and 21st century figures each of whom represents a cross section of literary, media, sports, government, and the private sector. Henrik stares at his computer while Alesha looks out at the gently falling snow. Each of them is struggling. The persons in question have a wide range of interests, personalities, followers, detractors, heights, weights, ethnicities, etc.

Then, Alesha states in a loud voice, "Each is known for his/her *legacy*!"

One of the persons was known for her unadulterated usage of the most-vile language in various media forums. Another woman was known for starting a line of footwear, and the profits were all given to charitable causes. Another person was known for his ability to take four pieces of anything and turn them into invaluable artwork. Henrik exclaims, "Of course. That's it!" Each person was well-known, and created a *permanent record of reliability*, albeit notorious in more than one case. You could *trust* there would be a predictable behavior. Behaviors established a legacy.

Six months ago, if anyone would have told me I would be co-authoring a book, I would have told her to have her head examined. Write a book? Are you kidding? I don't read books. When it comes to reading, I am lazy. I don't even read instructions (could be a guy thing).

So, why even think about writing a book?

It was an outgrowth of my wanting to leave a *legacy* to my children, to my friends and colleagues, other co-workers, supervisors, bosses, superiors, and maybe most importantly, to those who I will never meet.

I can leave memorabilia and other things to my heirs, but really, in most cases, those are virtually worthless, can get lost or displaced, and generally are only meaningful to me. But words? Thoughts? Actions? Those can and should be meaningful and lasting; i.e. a legacy. Today, perhaps more than ever, some might argue legacies are harder to discern while others could ostensibly argue legacies are made and dissolved just as quickly as table salt being added to water. This could be due to collisions of differing values or even lack of common understanding among various groups of people.

The reasons are irrelevant; however, *the legacy of creating a legacy* could be more important than it ever has been. And, perhaps egotistically, I wanted to be known for something positive after I am gone.

Knowing I would need help, guidance, and mentorship from a subject matter expert, I naturally reached out to my long-time friend, trusted agent, former US Air Force co-worker, and overall great guy, Bruce Goeas. I've known Bruce for over 35 years, and he and I have a common bond and heritage in so many ways. We work well together, and he has always been there for me. His first book, an immediate success and the beacon which illuminated this journey, *Where Fear Fails*, captivated me from the start and all the way through to the end.

When I talked to Bruce about the notion of co-authoring a book, there was no hesitation on his part. He said, "Let's do it!" We had never discussed a joint venture before in this area, so we were off to the races and not looking back.
Before I knew it, Bruce had the title registered (even got an ISBN number...whatever that is!), and he was demanding inputs from me. I mused, "Is it too late to turn back?"

So, here we are.

This book is aimed primarily at those who are just entering the workforce, those in mid-career, and those, much like Bruce and me, entering the golden years. Don't get me wrong…each of us has many years of productive work years left, and each of us also has the benefit of many lessons learned, and we want to collectively share those, in a legacy sort of way, such that we impart knowledge we feel, based upon decades of career ups and downs, can be used non-generationally regardless of any other criteria.

Legacy Play begins with a shared understanding and a look at an approach for creating your end state or goal. This chapter also provides several types of legacies.

Next is a deeper dive exploring requisite components of a legacy: Values (Chapter Two), Exhilarating Purpose (Chapter Three), Trust and Trusted Agents (Chapter Four), and Uniquely Designed (Chapter Five).

A discussion about Taking Inventory (Chapter Six) provides information and exercises related to the five elements of a lasting legacy.

The book concludes with a look at the impact of your legacy (Chapter Seven), the Cost of Doing Nothing if you choose not to pursue your legacy (Chapter Eight), and some Final Thoughts in (Chapter Nine).

In most of the chapters, the topic covered will be augmented by my perspectives as someone in a senior leadership role who has helped others, in some small part, I hope, craft his/her own legacy, while actively pursuing my own. There will be take-aways, aka legacies, which we hope will resonate within the reader.

Finally, Bruce and I hope you find this book useful and one you, as a reader, can use as a reference regardless of your chosen path, whether you are 25 or 75. We hope Legacy Play helps the reader think about his/her legacy creation, and ultimately, about the legacy.

May you find some meaning in what you are about to read. If not, my personal experience is books make excellent paperweights!

Respectfully,

Steve Darr
Kenmore, WA
July 10, 2018

Chapter One

Element 1

Legacy in Perspective

"All good men and women must take responsibility to create legacies that will take the next generation to a level we could only imagine."

Jim Rohn

One year ago, Steve and I met in Palm Desert, California. We were both going through significant life and career transitions, and some time had passed since our last face-to-face meeting.

After briefly catching up on family, friends, and life in general, the discussion turned to our lives, travels, and experiences. This naturally segued into thoughts about the good we have hopefully left in our wake. A seed was planted that day.

Some time passed, and life took over. This is a consistent pattern, and we always seem to reconnect when the timing is right. After exchanging a few emails, we decided it was time to chat again and we scheduled a phone conversation.

Steve may have been a bit surprised by my quick agreement and desire to get started writing this book. You see, the seed had grown into a sapling over the course of the past year, and the timing of his request could not have been more perfectly timed.

The result is a blueprint to help anyone (regardless of your generation) craft and deliver the legacy she/he is designed to create. Similar to a play a coach uses to plan, practice for, and win a game; this would be a **Legacy Play.**

So, let's get started….

A natural starting point for any play is to ensure a shared understanding or meaning.

I learned a long time ago even if I have known someone for many years, have pure intent, and care deeply about them, I still finish their sentences incorrectly. Guessing Steve and my wife could both provide confirmation here.

Consequently, let's start with a common definition of Legacy.

Legacy:

something transmitted by or received from an ancestor or predecessor or from the past

(Merriam-Webster)

This definition was chosen for our shared meaning because it references a transfer of 'something' from someone who came before us. The purpose of the Legacy Play is to help you determine the 'something' you want to leave behind and the 'someone' you want to receive it.

In the month's following the Palm Desert meeting, I found myself reflecting on a simple question:

How does thinking about what might be written or said about your legacy help you define it?

The question's origin is a CEO I once worked with who addressed every new hire orientation for his company. He talked about the company, its goals, and the role he hoped the new associates would play in their mutual success.

He then said every employee in the company, including the CEO, would encounter situations when deliverables would place them under great stress. During those times leaders or clients might ask them to make decisions or take actions resulting in an uneasy feeling in their gut. When those times occur, he asked them to ask one question and one question only:

"Would Bob, our CEO, want to read about this decision on the front page of the Wall Street Journal?"

It became known as his "Front Page Ethics Test." While in this context, the question is aimed at making an ethical decision, the 'front page' approach also provides a great way to think about your legacy. It moves your thought process to what you would like to have said or written about your life's endeavor. Additionally, it provides an opportunity to envision what success looks like for your chosen legacy.

As you begin to explore and craft your legacy, ask what you would like to be written or said when your work is complete. Some examples follow.

What might it look or sound like?

- Articles and news reports highlight the technologies, products, or medicines you invented and their positive impact on others' lives.

- People in your community are discussing or recognizing your service to your community or society.

- History records your efforts to change the world, leaving it better than you found and something of great worth for generations to come.

- Someone gives you credit for believing in him before he could believe in himself. Full credit is given for providing the coaching, mentoring, or teaching that changed his world.

- You thoughtfully connect with things, places, family, and others creating memories for loved ones to keep and hold for generations.

Asking what might be written or said provides a glimpse into your legacy and what form it might take.

Which legacy type resonates most with your vision?

Career Contribution

This form of legacy involves a life-long career which impacts others. It might be a career that sets an example for one's children or grandchildren. It could entail working until the end of one's life creating or providing something that changes other's lives. The key here is that you will build your legacy in a career environment. Typically, this form involves a life's work with continued contribution for an entire lifetime.

When I think about this type of legacy, names such as Andy Grove, Jonas Salk, Steve Jobs, Pierre and Marie Curie, and Alexander Graham Bell come to mind. Individuals or teams that made their contributions in their chosen fields.

This form is for those of you who receive strange looks from strangers and friends alike when you proclaim "I don't see myself ever retiring." Many of you feel that your work is not done yet.

Do you feel the greatest contribution you can make is to continue your life's work?

An important point about forms or types of legacies will probably surface a couple of times, so let's address it here. In reading this, some might be thinking there are many examples of people who made their mark in the corporate environment, who gave a great deal to their communities, or to charitable organizations, or pursued causes that helped the world. All true. As we seek to define our legacies, we will see overlap with other forms. Our endeavor here is to define the primary legacy you will focus on, while acknowledging it will most likely touch some of the other types.

Community Service

Unlike the names mentioned in the Career Contribution section you may not have heard of Christian Thomas Lee, Neilesh Patel DDS, or Carly Yoost. They are a musician, dentist, and a Tech CEO.

Lee is a Points of Light Award recipient for bringing music and the arts to inner city youth.

Dr. Patel is a Jefferson Public Service Award winner (under age 35 category) for his work using the internet to provide healthcare for over one million people worldwide.

Carly Yoost is a Lifetime Honoree--Presidential Volunteer Service Award winner (individual category) for her work as the CEO of the non-profit Child Rescue Coalition (CRC) where she converted her for-profit software solution into a community service solution for finding lost children. Carly Yoost takes no salary for her work with CRC.

Christian, Neilesh, and Carly are just a few of the millions of people who have leveraged their experience and background to pursue a legacy of community service. Efforts to help others less fortunate are being initiated by former businesspeople, athletes, young people who are wise beyond their years, faith-based leaders, actors and actresses, youth coaches, and citizens from all walks of life who have been called to serve.

Those pursuing a Community Service legacy build homes, deliver food, fight online bullying, serve the elderly, protect our neighborhoods, support our troops, fight illiteracy, and address millions of other needs.

Is there an unaddressed need in your community that you are called to address?

Changing the World

We already discussed the two largest generations and their mantra to Change the World. While this made for a great reason to express concern for certain causes for many, the concern stops shortly after the Facebook campaign, protest march, or boycott. The energy wanes and people go back to their lives, families, friends, and the drudgery of everyday life. However, for some, the cause is so important, massive, and all-consuming it just has to be taken on.

As we write this book, in an eight-hour span Gina Haspel was named the first female Director of the CIA and Stacey Cunningham was named as the first female to be named President of the New York Stock Exchange. Both started their careers in the organizations they now head (Haspel as a CIA Operator and Cunningham as an intern on the floor of the exchange). By all counts, each is more than qualified based on their knowledge, talents, and experience.

As Haspel pointed out she had great mentors coming up through the ranks and 'she stands on the shoulders of the women who came before her.' No doubt a legacy created by the brave suffragettes of the late 18th and early 19th centuries, and the woman's rights activists of the late 20th century. The legacy was paid for with imprisonment, hunger strikes, and physical abuse.

For those who wondered why we chose to address Community Service and Changing the World separately, the suffragettes struggle provides the logic. While both forms of service require sacrifices, Community Service is typically lauded and recognized in positive ways. World Changing activities/campaigns often are met with derision and violence.
Those called to change the world envision legacies that are big, bold, and fraught with peril. These causes are pursued by true believers, with good intentions, and pure motives.

Their legacies cover the full gambit of a changed world:

- Saving whales, seals, and dolphins
- Potable water everywhere in the world
- Death with dignity
- Mothers protecting their children against drunk drivers
- Equal access to the American Dream through access to technology for every child
- Practical education ensuring enough plumbers, electricians, mechanics, and other craftspeople for the foreseeable future

The incredible people who pursue such legacies are often unique, energized, obsessed, and see their vision well before others are ready for them. Their works tend to be high risk and when they come to fruition, high reward. Many note they just had to do something.

Is there a cause or change that you just can't ignore any longer and must pursue?

Tending to the Heart

While this last legacy type may be generational, it probably is true in each generation there will be some who will look back at their life's journey and say there are some things and relationships that represent unfinished business. Stressful events, busy schedules, work requirements, and frequent travel that robbed precious time from people, activities, and hobbies.

I have a dear friend who by all counts has had a brilliant career. She worked hard, gave selflessly of herself and time, a true company person. Along the way relationships, time for self, anniversary and birthday celebrations, and vacations all took a backseat to her dedicated service to the companies she worked for.

My hope for her Career Legacy Play recently was dashed.

You see, retirement crept up on her unexpectedly. She woke one morning with no work tasks, a free calendar, and boxes full of stuff from a desk in an office she no longer occupied. Awake with no place to go.

Instead of focusing on all she had accomplished and the legacy she had left for the future generations working for her previous employers, she drifted to sadness about what was sacrificed along the way. The good news is that she reached out to her small circle of friends. We rallied to the cause and began asking questions and exploring her future. What has she always wanted to do and see? What relationships would she pursue now that time and schedule are no longer an issue? She quickly noted she wanted a soulmate (not necessarily a husband).

Additionally, she said she had always wanted to visit Europe and places where her ancestors were born. And, she had always wanted to take up painting. Her goals and desires were always there along the way. They just needed increased priority on her task list.

Like most legacies, focus can make all of the difference. Since tending to her heart's desires became the number one focus she has painted and sold some paintings at a local wine and art fair. She has become the Aunt and Sister she had longed to be for many years. Following a trip to Europe, she became a season ticket holder for a local opera theatre. And, she attends the opera with a friend who she loves spending time with, without having to file joint taxes.

Needless-to-say, this type of legacy can be a bit tricky. Often times people think it is selfish for them to pursue. The reality is that this is about unfinished business. Relationships, hobbies, travel, mindfulness, or time to pursue a talent are victims of a lack of attention. In most cases other requirements have taken up the space and time. And now it is time to place a priority on setting an example and being present for you children and grandchildren or to pursue those things you were uniquely designed to do.

We have friends who have joined a small theatre group and are acting for the first time. Others are taking up musical instruments and surprised by their talent. Others now produce most of the vegetables they eat. In each case they have expanded their circle of friends and reconnected with family because these activities can all be shared.

What unfinished relationship, activity, or talent are you called to re-engage?

Steve's Perspective-Pitfalls or Landmines

What are the potential roadblocks to pursuing your legacy?

Ego

Believe it or not, it ain't about you, baby! (This statement is aimed directly at myself).

I recall an individual who Bruce and I worked with very closely. I don't remember Steven for his stature, or intelligence, or his polished, professional appearance. But, I do remember him for one, unfailing trait: his selflessness. No matter what, Steven ALWAYS, ALWAYS, ALWAYS asked what he could do to help. Steven would be heard saying, "What needs to be done?" or, "What do you want me to do?" I recently saw a picture of Steven that I hadn't seen in decades. In my mind, I see him asking others how he could serve them. Steven has a legacy. Do you? If not, why?

If you think you should create a legacy so you can be 'revered' in the future, I would ask you to re-evaluate your motive(s). I personally believe ego is the number one detractor to servitude and leadership. It has been my continuing observation those in leadership roles who are humble yield a better executive persona than those who are not. I have seen those in positions of power, especially on Boards of Directors, whose egos far outstrip their capabilities and humanity. Don't fall into the trap that the higher you progress the less human you become. It is a long fall down.

Not caring

Apathy creeps into our personal and business lives. We show up. We do things from rote. We churn daily without caring. Tied to ego, and trust me, I speak from personal experience as I have personally struggled with this for decades, not caring is a recipe that leads to not wanting to do many things. And, one of those is the creation of a legacy....it leads to an environment in which one doesn't let the legacy even be born.

I draw our attention to J. J. Watt of the Houston Texans. J. J., by all counts, is a gifted pro football player. But, more importantly, he is creating a legacy of caring. Years from now, whether or not he makes the Hall of Fame, J. J. will be known for his caring and his philanthropic ways. Many of you will say he has the means to care, and that is true. But, look how many in our society have the means and NEVER exert the effort to care. Do you care?

You are never too old, nor too young, to craft your legacy

I view my legacy as a part of my DNA. What I want to be remembered for may, and most likely will, be different from what you might want to have as a legacy. I believe it to be a smaller part of your personal brand.

When I reflect on my life, I wish I had given more time and thought into creating a personal brand. Ah, there is Steve Darr. He has a strong moral compass. He can be trusted. He tried to do what is right and fight injustice. Unfortunately, for too many decades, my ego obfuscated what was and is truly important. Now, as I approach my eighth decade on this planet, I finally know what is important...for me!

I challenge each of you to reflect on what your brand should be. What does it say about you? Regardless if you deal with difficult children, a stressed and degraded work environment, or sit in traffic for hours on end, at the end of the day, how will others remember you? Your brand will define those memories.

Steve's Thought Box

What steps can you take TODAY to begin to make your legacy a reality?

1. Look inward

2. Ask for feedback from others

3. Be selfless

4. Act locally (introspectively) and think globally (caring for others)

5. Create a brand that is you and is a hallmark of what your legacy should be. It's a part of your DNA.

6. Repeat steps 1-5.

Chapter Two

Element 2

Values and Non-Negotiables

"It's not hard to make decisions when you know what your values are."

Roy Disney

Success Happens When Your Values are in Sync

'What do you want to be when you grow up?'

It's an age-old question. Parents, grandparents, uncles, and aunts all engaged in the game; often times hoping your response fits what they would consider admirable or worthy of note.

Needless-to-say, my Jesuit educated dad and mother with Irish heritage took great pleasure when they discovered me saying mass when I was about six.

Imagine six-year old me with a turtle neck under a bathrobe, towel over the coffee table (a fitting altar), paper cup for a chalice, vanilla wafer 'hosts,' and GI Joe and stuffed animals all in their 'pews.' Most likely an eloquent sermon, by six-year old standards, followed.

This career option stayed intact until I discovered priests can't marry. Strangely enough, about the same time I discovered girls in high school.

The interesting twist is that while the title or role changed over the years, my values did not.

For example, I pride myself on being that person anyone could share their worries, concerns, or woes with. Although painfully humbled anytime someone honors me or singles me out, I love being in front of a classroom or on a stage. For me, nothing is more energizing than sharing what I believe or have learned, hopefully helping others grow in the process.

Other values became part of my DNA as well. For example, fighting for those I perceived to be the underdog. Or, trying to display unconditional loyalty to my friends, both furry and human. There is also my belief that integrity is the only thing we have at the end of our life and that integrity is most accurately displayed when no one is watching. And, finally, I believe in giving gratitude daily for all of my blessings, no matter how my day turns out.

The values I cherish are ever-present and always front of mind.

While my life as a priest was interrupted, my desire to serve others has lived on. Military service, teaching, coaching, and consultative selling were all connected to my values and the concept of serving others.

When my values are in sync with the values of the organization, company, or leaders I serve, success is always the byproduct. However, when there is a 'values clash' a different outcome typically occurs.

When Values Clash, Failure is Close Behind

As the years rolled along others provided feedback on where they believed I should be headed and what I should aspire to be. Some advice worked out well and some did not. In every situation those who provided the advice had pure intent and my best interest in mind.

The challenge with a vision or purpose crafted by someone else is that it may not take your value set into account.

For example, while serving in the military, many well-meaning senior officers discussed my pathway to becoming a General Officer. Their input was well-meaning and definitely was what they thought was in my best interest. Following my ten years on active duty, many of the sales leaders I worked for discussed my path to becoming the number one salesperson in the company.

Here's the rub: being a high visibility leader or an organization's top salesperson directly clashes with the value I place on humility and not taking credit for another's hard work. These pursuits were neither important or motivational for me. Consequently, at an important crossroad in my Air Force career, I accepted an assignment that others pointed out would remove me from contention for becoming a General Officer. Additionally, in 20/20 hindsight, I think my consultative sales career is littered with examples of when I walked right up to the recognition line and then pulled hard on the reins.

It is important to note, there are others for whom the roles listed above are in direct alignment with what they value. That is neither good or bad because as we discussed in Chapter One, legacies take many forms. It is also important to point out, for me, writing this book with Steve is driven in part by the knowledge that while we have many shared values, our chosen career paths are different and provide different perspectives. Our career paths are also nicely aligned with our unique value set.

It probably is apparent by now that I believe there is a strong correlation between your core values and the success of your legacy. This belief about the values-success connection is based on some foundational thoughts that warrant exploration.

Ensure it is Your Legacy

As noted earlier, there are plenty of well-meaning people who just can't wait to help you craft your purpose, path, or legacy. We have also established that due to our values, talents, and motivations some paths to establishing our legacy are less desirable than others. Consequently, it is very important to validate that the legacy you are pursuing is in fact your own.

It is human nature to seek approval and want others to accept your actions. This need for approval is also what makes our dreams more likely to represent what our parents, friends, or bosses would approve of than what we would create for ourselves.

Please don't get me wrong. We all ask whether someone we value, respect, or love would be proud of us or support what we are doing. It is just that a successful legacy must be values driven and require you to bring your best self to the task. Owning something always takes on a different significance than renting something. So, you must own your legacy.

Authentic Self

From my perspective owning your legacy requires that you bring your authentic self to the purpose or task at hand. Unless your value set includes 'winning at all costs' or 'doing whatever it takes,' pretending to be someone you are not seems to be at odds with successfully crafting your legacy.

It appears to me that over the years when I tried to be someone I am not mediocrity followed. When I was less than honest with myself about how some job, task, or transition fit my purpose in life, it did not produce much more than a learning experience I would hopefully not soon repeat.

As previously noted, it is my firm belief that when all is said and done the only thing that I will be able to hold onto is my top value, integrity. I have case-based reasoning that says my body and mind will at some point begin to fail. Additionally, there will come a time when money no longer serves a purpose in my life. At the end I will be left with my integrity in its highest form--being honest with myself about who I truly am and the impact my authentic self has had on the people and world I leave behind.

Compromising on Values

Linked to being your authentic self is the concept of compromising on values. Can you be your authentic self and compromise on your core values?

My take is that our values provide the true north for who we are. Our values are steadfast and consistent. The only thing that waivers or changes is our commitment to them. When we compromise on our values it is difficult to truly be our authentic self.

Legacy and Passion

Steve can attest to my warped sense of curiosity. He has more than once been the subject of my questioning. One of my favorite inquiries is to ask friends and family "When was the last time you sprang out of bed in the morning?" For me this question provides insight into whether someone is living their dream or just going through the motions addressing life's many 'need to' and 'must have' demands.

I can't help but wonder if anyone can think of some great fete they accomplished without a passion for the accomplishment and its result or impact. It is passion that provides the energy and courage to start the journey. Passionate language is at the heart of getting others to see your vision and join in. And I am absolutely certain that when the going gets tough without passion the effort will wane and the legacy will die.

Years of experience have shown, both in my life and in observing others, that if you are pursuing something that you own, that is in alignment with your values, and clear in its purpose you will spring out of bed each morning to make it happen.

Values are the foundation, passion is the fuel, and clarity of purpose is the roadmap that transforms your legacy from hope to reality. We will explore clarity of purpose in the next chapter.

Steve's Perspective-Pitfalls or Landmines

What are the potential consequences of not honoring your values in pursuit of your legacy?

Trust

Your legacy must be your own. What is most important to you and those you wish to value your legacy? Is it integrity as Bruce has mentioned? Is it honesty? Is it trust? For me, it is trust, but it has not always been so.

How many of you can honestly say you work for someone you completely and undeniably trust 100%? When I reflect on working for someone I completely trusted, I think back to my first supervisor when I left the US Air Force and went to work for Honeywell in West Covina, California. I worked for a gruff old curmudgeon, Bob Brodman. He had virtually no social skills, was an ex-USAF fighter pilot who lived a hard life, had an incredible work ethic which, to my observation, no one else could ever match, and, at the end of the day, ALWAYS knew his place in the organization. And, he made sure that I, and the rest of his subordinates, knew the same. But the one trait Bob always conveyed was that of trust. He never withheld his mid-course corrections, gave praise in public and chastised in private. When he said something, you could take it to the bank…and it would earn interest.

How does one quantify trust? I believe it to be very subjective. Can you trust someone immediately? When you walk onto a plane, do you trust the flight crew is fully trained, sober, and capable of handling any emergency? When you undergo surgery, are you confident…do you TRUST….the surgeon and her team know what procedure is scheduled and competent to carry it out?

Trust is earned, at least to my way of thinking, over time. That time is a function of each situation, and there is not one set answer.

How do you engender trust? Are you able to have difficult conversations with those around you in a manner which is respectful? Do you look those in the eye when you converse? Are you honest with yourself?

There are so many traits which could be pivotal to your legacy. Is trust one of them? If not, I would ask you to extensively reflect on whether it should be. Surely, integrity and honesty are important, and perhaps for you, one of those, or even a different trait, may be more important than trust as a legacy play.

Don't get me wrong. Trust does NOT imply you will always be accurate. It DOES imply that when situations or conditions CHANGE, you, as a legacy holder of trust, a trustee of trust, will be able to adapt to the situation, and those who hold you in esteem will say, "Even though our plans changed, I trusted Garrett because of the manner in which he handled a similar situation in the past."

What is the pitfall?

As with anything, complacency. Have you worked for someone you don't trust, or if you did, and something happened, you lost that trust for her? Have you had a partner in something, perhaps on a sports team for whom you had a great deal of trust but lost it? Stories are plentiful of key athletes losing trust of their peers for recurring instances of lack of trust. Obviously, so are state and federal governments a fertile ground of trust implosion.

As with parenting, consistent application is key. Don't waiver. Could you put your 'life story' on the front of the New York Times and not be nervous?

Steve's Thought Box

What steps can you take to ensure there is a match between your values and your chosen path?

1. What are YOUR values and behaviors? Do you portray a façade which doesn't really reflect the real you? How do you measure yourself against your value system?

2. If someone were to interview you on your value and behavior protocols, would you be proud? If not, is it too late to change? I would challenge each of you, as I challenge myself continually, to re-evaluate YOUR unique situation and to modify, as appropriate, to reflect the real 'you'. I can guarantee the person I was in the 1970s is NOT the person I am today. In some ways, I am better, but there are other areas in which I constantly drive and strive to improve.

3. Be humble. Ask for feedback from trusted agents. Regardless of what you want your legacy to be, don't be afraid to realize you need help in crafting your legacy. Ultimately, it will be your legacy to execute, but the more inputs you receive, the better, the more refined, the more in-sync it will be.

4. Do you work for an employer who offers 360s? If you do, analyze what those indicate. Put a self-improvement plan in place. Look for trends as the years pass and honestly measure yourself. No one will ever reach 'perfection', but the goal is to continuously improve.

Chapter Three

Element 3

Exhilarating Purpose

"True happiness…is not attained through self-gratification, but through fidelity to a worthy purpose."

Helen Keller

On Purpose:

the object toward which one strives or for which something exists; an aim or goal

(The Free Dictionary, by Farlex)

You Know

Recently I met a young man who represents an interesting example of the concept of knowing his purpose from a very young age.

Having believed for many years that we know on some level at a very young age what our purpose is, I was intrigued when this young man's mother and sister told a story of him ordering duck and buffalo in restaurants as young as 8 years old. They shared how the wait staff normally responded with an 'Isn't that cute' statement of some sort. And, how they loved to see the server's face when this young man gave his culinary perspective on the dish when the meal was completed.

While attending college the young man chose to work in restaurants. Didn't matter what role he took on, he spent the time learning how to run a restaurant and create incredible dishes. Fast forward, today this young 26-year old owns three restaurants and has two more in the works. By all accounts he is a phenomenal success. He is on purpose and has known his purpose for a very long time.

This is just the latest example. I have met future Air Force officers who knew they would be pilots at 6 or 7-years old. I have a younger brother who could draw a straight line freehand as young as 5-years old who is now an influential architect. Over time, there have been counselors, teachers, coaches, musicians, and artists.

As more and more data points were added through the years, I became obsessed with the concept of knowing what our purpose in life is and how powerful it can be when we are doing things **on purpose**.

My search led me to the works of a team of Gallup scientists which included Tom Rath, Marcus Buckingham, and Dr. Donald Clifton. Their *Strength Finder* books and surveys, based on 40 years of Gallup research, reinforced my belief that we have certain innate strengths.

The Gallup research, coupled with the works of Richard Leider (*The Power of Purpose*) and Rick Warren (*The Purpose Driven Life*) reinforced the idea that when we are leveraging our intrinsic strengths good things happen and **we know** we are on path. No doubt you have heard and seen examples of people who clearly are using their natural talents and are on purpose.

When someone is on path certain phrases tend to surface:

"She is in the zone."

"It is in his wheel house."

"She is in the flow."

"He's a natural at this."

Being on purpose is also visible in the way people act, interact, move, and produce. Like a great long-distance runner, when someone is fulfilling his or her purpose instincts, talent, and muscle memory take over. What is a struggle for many looks almost effortless for those in the zone.

So, how do you know when you are on path?

Proof Statement #1: You spring out of bed

Have you noticed problems almost always seem worse at night and less daunting in the morning? If things are almost always brighter in the morning it is hard to fathom how, being on purpose, we could sleep in or slowly roll out of bed.

When you are on purpose you can't wait to get started each day. You spring into action and focus on results. The focus is rarely on you or some other individual, it is on your legacy, its beneficiaries, and on its impact.

For anyone who has been welcomed home by a faithful pet, the behavior is similar. It doesn't matter how long you have been gone there is always fanfare and a great deal of energy expended. I have friends who are fighting Alzheimer's, pursuing affordable housing for the bay area's elderly population, and reconnecting with their adult children by taking joint vacations to exotic places. I can honestly say that engaging them before an event or prior to a trip looks very similar to the greeting I receive every time I return home.

This is quite different from an existence where you pursue frivolous daily activities to avoid dealing with mundane work-related tasks. A bias for productive action is graphically different from busy work, surviving the day, or counting the hours until the weekend.

What purpose were you pursuing the last time you sprang out of bed and engaged life with vigor?

Proof Statement #2: You tell anyone who will listen

Do you recall that birthday or other special occasion when you received that present you so badly wanted? Did you work the neighborhood showing anyone who would pay attention? Did you show the kids next door, the neighbor mowing his lawn, the neighborhood postal worker, or the local dog walker? If it fit in your bed, did you sleep with it for a week?

That is what it feels like when your purpose is clear and you are on purpose. When a cause, a person, or a community is of greatest importance you want to tell anyone who will listen. Your efforts might save a life, feed a child, or help a first-generation college graduate and you can't wait to tell people about it and get others involved.

I mentioned one of our friends who is actively involved in the fight to eliminate Alzheimer's. I will never forget the day that we donned our brand new purple t-shirts and walked the streets of San Jose with thousands of other people sharing the cause. The fact is that without our friend spreading the word we would not have even known about the event. She told her church, distributed fliers, and on our Sunday walks told anyone we came across about the San Jose Alzheimer's Walk. Yes, she told anyone who would listen and is responsible for hundreds of participants that were there that day.

When you need help you will ask anyone in earshot. When you experience a victory, you want to share the triumph with everyone from Facebook friends to the barista at the coffee shop. If you are clear about your purpose, what impact it will have, and who it benefits you will want to tell the world.

Who do you tell about your legacy?

Proof Statement #3: Persistence in difficult times

'May you live in interesting times.'
(English blessing or Chinese curse)

While there is some debate about the origins of the phrase above, there is no debate that when interesting times surface dedication to one's purpose can be tested. One sure sign that you are on purpose is your willingness to push through challenges and roadblocks when they arise.

A few years back a charitable organization I had been giving to for years ran into some challenges with bad press and lower rankings from some of the charity rating agencies. I could not help but wonder if the charity would survive and what impact their absence would have on the important people they served.

The organization promptly applied resources, time, and money to correcting the record and reviving its brand. The challenges were stubborn and took time and resources away from their core mission. However, the organization kept picking itself up noting that their cause was too important to walk away.

Persistence and focus helped the charity survive and then thrive. Retractions and apologies were offered by the press and rating agencies. The charity's high ratings returned and the organization got back to fulfilling its purpose.

When your legacy is on purpose and the cause great you will find the strength to push through the tough times and difficult situations.

When challenges and roadblocks surface is your purpose important enough to fight for?

Proof Statement #4: Fully leverages your best self

We are all a composite of our experiences, the knowledge we have acquired, the skills we have developed, and our innate personal traits. The concept of Best Self will be more deeply explored in Chapter 5: Uniquely Designed to Be and Do. So, for the purposes of this chapter let's briefly look at how a legacy on purpose leverages your best self.

For 44 years (1966-2010) Labor Day Weekend was synonymous with the Jerry Lewis MDA Telethon. For those of you not familiar with the MDA Telethon, it was a non-stop broadcast with Jerry Lewis as the host. Jerry was on camera for most of the telecast. He was physically and emotionally depleted by the end of the Telethon when he belted out his closing number, 'You will never walk alone.' It was his legacy and leveraged his very best self.

Jerry Lewis was a great comedian and performer. He was bright, funny, and was renowned for his physical humor. The long-term success of the MDA Telethon leveraged Jerry's innate talents as an entertainer and showman, his acquired negotiation and fundraising skills, and his love for the children he served. Bringing his passion and best self to bear, Jerry raised millions from small and large donors alike. His famous tote board and introduction of special contributors served as visual proof of the great research and good deeds his legacy provided. He gave his all until there was no more to give. His cause fully leveraged his best self.

Yes, we know when we are on purpose because it demands our best self.

Is your defined purpose buoyed by the experience, knowledge, skills, and personal traits you bring to bear?

Steve's Perspective--Pitfalls or Landmines

How does the lack of clarity impact the beneficiaries of your legacy?

You must define your future. Only you can truly do that. There is a number of different ways to do this. You could devise a personal strategic plan on where you want to be in x number of years. That plan would have specific milestones against which you measure yourself. If employed, you could have your people manager perform a 360 or similar on your so you could understand your areas of strength and improvements.

The point is you cannot go into the planning for creation of a legacy without a thorough understanding of who you are and where you want to be as you continue your life's journey. Had I done that many years ago, I am positive my life's path would have been much different. I recall my dad telling me right before he went to Southeast Asia to fly 352 combat sorties, "You need to determine what and who you want to be." He knew me better than I knew myself, and the answer took decades to solidify.

So, take some time to perform that self-evaluation. Get help from those you can count on. Define who and what you want to be by when.

Steve's Thought Box

What can you do to create and implement a purposeful legacy?

1. How do you leave the world a better place? It takes a continuing commitment to do so. Saying it and doing it are far apart. Maybe, it is similar to a New Year's resolution in which someone commits to a particular goal. And, perhaps, even more deeply, what is there that indicates what YOU want to do to make the world a better place really WILL leave it a better place. How does one define a 'better' place? Where the needs of the many outweigh the needs of the few?

   This is not a trivial thought. How do YOU define betterment? Not only does one have to define it for herself, but I also believe it needs refinement and consensus from those around her. Like climbing a mountain, it takes years of planning, preparation, and attempts. It doesn't happen overnight.

   And that, readers, is my encouragement to you in order to leave a legacy. For the reader who is younger, set the goal, then prepare a personal betterment plan to achieve that part of your legacy. For the older reader, you may not have the time to do as much preparation, but you have the benefit of years of trials and tribulations.

   Regardless of your age, there is SOMETHING each of us can do NOW to begin to craft a legacy.

2. How do you influence those around you? Is it done by consensus? Is it done in a vacuum? Have you ever worked with someone you admire? If so, what makes him admirable? Is it his honesty? Do you trust him? Does he have a strong work ethic? Perhaps, he exhibits all those, and more. From my experiences, the most effective legacy builders do so by covert and overt means. By covert, I mean virtually imperceptible. For example, the best influencers do so by asking probing questions. "What would you do?" or, "How would you handle this?" So, to take this to the next level, give some thought to how YOU can influence WITHOUT giving orders or direction. Your ability to influence and bolster whatever legacy you craft will be directly proportional to your ability to influence. It is an art and won't be complete overnight.

Chapter Four
Element 4
Trust and Trusted Agents

"Whoever is careless with the truth in small matters cannot be trusted with important matters."

Albert Einstein

Trust is a requisite for any Legacy

As we outlined this book, trust surfaced as a major issue for Steve. So, we added this chapter. Steve will share more on his passion around trust in a bit.

Trust seemed like a given to me, a ticket for entry for any legacy if you will. I envisioned readers reading the heading above, rolling their eyes and shouting 'Duh.' Then I was hit by a sudden attack of good judgment and several thoughts came to mind.

First, as the saying goes, common sense is not always common in complex organizations or complex relationships. Some times what appears to be obvious is hidden in plain sight.

Second, I am guessing most of us have been on a team or a committee where someone placed a different value on giving and earning trust than we did. In my experience, both as a team member and a consultant (observer), this normally produced mediocre results at best because human dynamics were impacted by a lack of trust.

Third, without trust each move, challenge, and decision has a cloud hanging over it. Is there pure intent? What are the motives behind each person's actions? Do they even believe in what we are doing here, or just giving lip service?

So, while this may elicit a 'Duh', it clearly deserves a mention.

Trust is a requisite for any successful legacy. Now, onto Steve's thoughts on this important issue.

While we were writing this book, Bruce asked me via text, "Do you trust me?" Obviously, the answer was yes…but WHY was the answer yes. Bruce has always been there for me for over three decades. He listens. He doesn't judge. He is patient. Sorry, ladies…he is taken!!

Anyway, I had to come up with one verifiable moment that flipped the switch from 'TBD' to TRUST.

One night during the summer of 1985, Bruce, his wife, Chris, and I had dinner in Santa Barbara. We were stationed at Vandenberg AFB, California, and I had already put in my separation paperwork to voluntarily resign my commission from the US Air Force. We were in separate cars. As we 'sped' back towards Vandenberg going north on US101 near Gaviota, I got stopped for speeding. Bruce was trailing (I deplore being behind anyone in traffic regardless of who it might be) and saw all this happen in front of him. Rather than continue on to Vandenberg, Bruce stopped to await my fate. Many others would have continued on, and we would have joined up on a future date. But not Bruce. He wanted to make certain I was all right, and that I didn't need any help (and maybe not going to jail!!).

At that moment, I knew I could trust Bruce, regardless of the situation. His behavior at that moment formed the cornerstone of our relationship, and since that night, has been rock steady…*reliable…predictable*.

Trust Defined

Trust.   What is trust?   It's a verb, and it is also a noun. Regardless, it is important, and I feel it may be the NUMBER ONE discriminator for me as I finalize and fine-tune my personal legacy.

How many of us have had bosses, supervisors, managers, colleagues, co-workers, and direct reports who failed to live the trust each of us put in them? I know I have lived that, and I imagine many of you have as well. Without trust, everything else falls apart. Trust is the foundational element upon which everything else sits. Erode trust, and all above it is at risk.

And, why might trust be important, perhaps paramount, in establishing a lasting legacy? All one needs to do is to watch any cable news outlet to see continuing stories of how trust has been broken by so many.   Entertainment.   Sports. Government.   Military. All these sectors, and so many more, are rife with examples of people not being trustworthy. Then, after some time for reflection, the violator, in many cases, pleads for forgiveness, perhaps claiming influence by some factor, and with time passage, the incident seemingly vanishes from our memories.   But does it?

So, what is trust?

Is it always being honest?

Is it always being right?

Just what is it?

I contend trust is the act of being *reliable*, first, last, and always.

Trust and Reliability

My parents came from different economic upbringings. My dad was essentially headed to an orphanage at the tender age of three had his paternal grandparents not stepped in to rescue him. Can you imagine, I cannot, being given up for adoption because neither of your parents wanted you? Talk about a petri dish that could lead to not trusting anyone. Yet, that didn't occur. After leaving 'home,' my dad headed to Detroit to work for General Motors, enlisted in the US Army Air Corps, put himself through one of the most intense engineering disciplines at the University of Colorado to include getting his PhD in Aeronautical Engineering, served this country for 31 years, and, perhaps above all with the able assistance of my mom, created a stable home environment for our family.

What is the common theme? Reliability. Under what many, at that time in the 1930s would have considered duress, my dad honed his reliability trait.

My mom, on the other hand, grew up in a family of considerable means. Her dad built and operated two restaurants in Greeley, Colorado. Her mom was a stay-at-home provider. Yet, for reasons not pertinent to this discussion, the nurturing of her brother befell her. At a very young age, my mom, by necessity, had to create an environment of trust for her brother. She HAD to be there.

Again, the common theme is reliability. If one creates a reliable framework, does that lead to being trustworthy? I think it does. You may disagree.

Let's look at some other, personal examples.

I have previously mentioned my first supervisor at Honeywell. Bob was a gruff, ex-fighter pilot. Those who reported to him may not have liked his message and how he delivered it, but, one could always count on him being honest. Reliable.

In my senior roles with a variety of companies, I have made some really good hires, and, on the other hand, had some clunkers. There is a variety of traits I consider a good hire to possess. One is the ability to put her in front of your most demanding customer without hesitation.

Many years ago, I was leading a failure investigation for one of my company's products. Product had been fielded, and a recall was looming. That recall had the potential to cost the company many millions of dollars and an incalculable amount in reputation with a customer of untold import. We were deep into the investigation. The customer was very unhappy with our progress, the potential impact to its *reliability* standing with its customer, and our customer's customer was on site for this particular status meeting. It was a big deal.

During the meeting, one of our engineers was discussing the design of the electrical circuit in question and said, "Well, we knew we had a design issue when we designed it, but we elected not to do anything about it. We didn't think it would be a problem." After picking myself up from the floor, I asked for a break so we could re-group.

As it turned out, after many weeks of engineering analysis, testing, and a whole lot of cost, we didn't have a product performance issue because there was sufficient margin in the design (we didn't know that during the design phase of the effort). However, that engineer's one statement created a huge ripple effect through the company that translated into having everything we did be brought into question. It literally took more than five years to recover.

Did I ever trust that engineer again? I think the answer is obvious. After that, one of the initiatives I undertook was to develop an internal training program on HOW to talk to customers. And, that led to my modifying the one internal question I ask myself when I am thinking about hiring someone. "Could I put this person in front of the most-demanding customer, inquirer...whatever, and not worry?" While that is a good discriminator, it isn't the only one, and, unfortunately, it has proven to be less than reliable for me. As a result, my trust in my protocols has eroded.

Trust.

Are you thinking about this in terms of your legacy?

Trusted Agents

If you are in a position of leadership, those reporting to you and those to whom you report will need to have a great deal of trust in you. Are you ready?

Trust: Subordinates

The previous paragraphs have addressed subordinates, and by that term, I mean people either directly or indirectly, organizationally, reporting to you. Let me expand on this relationship.

When I was a Minuteman Missile Combat Crew Commander, I was responsible for a number of things. The professionalism of my crew. The trust the nation put in my crew to carry out directives from the National Command Authorities. And, for the conduct of the personnel assigned to the Launch Control Facility...those individuals 'upstairs' who were the security forces assigned. Even though we were downstairs in the Launch Control Center without any immediate means to detect what was going on upstairs and in our assigned flight of ten missiles, we had to trust those assigned personnel. I learned at an early professional age to trust. I am sure each of you has similar stories of trusting those you barely or even didn't know.

Of all the various groups, peers, supervisors, or subordinates, I personally believe trust of your subordinates may be grossly under-rated.

One day, whether you are a mid-level manager or a senior executive, the trust you have established with someone in your echelon will be tested, and you will not be there to intervene. Build trust early and nurture it. Test it. If it doesn't hold up, immediately put actions in place to strengthen it. If it means making a change, do so as quickly as possible. Your continued success will be highly dependent upon the trust you build with your team whether they are direct reports or others over which you have significant influence.

Trust: Supervisors

What would you do if your boss said, "I promise!", and that promise never materialized? This has happened to me, and it hurts. From that instant, no future promises are certain, are they? Everything that person says to you in the future is tainted with the possibility of unreliability. The trust meter, if it ever was, will never again be pegged. How you handle that is outside the scope of this book; however, Bruce and I would ask you to deeply reflect on loss of trust for your supervisor. Will your future work be compromised? Will you give your all to your employer? To those around you? And, what if you start to 'tell all' to your colleagues? Then, your reputation could potentially be impugned. Loss of trust for your supervisor has far-reaching and a potentially devastating impact.

Trust: Peers

Your peers are constantly monitoring you on how you interact with your superiors, them, and those who report to you. If one of those stakeholders detects a chink in your trust armor, then, there is the possibility of translation into how you are viewed. Having been around the block more than once, do you want someone, anyone, to answer a question about your trust ethic with, "Well, Jane has some trust issues with her staff."

Trust: Self

Do you trust yourself? Do you say what you are going to do and then do it? Could you put your life on the front page of the Wall Street Journal and not be sorry you did so?

Start by evaluating where you are in self-trust.

Trust: Recruiters

I want to take a few moments to target a particular subject near and dear to me, and this is aimed primarily at those more-senior managers/leaders who engage talent recruitment via head-hunters. Also, it pertains to any one being recruited. I have a great deal of passion about this subject, and I think it needs to be addressed here in the Trust section.

As most know, there are two main recruiting groups: contingency and retained. Although not entirely true, generally, contingency recruiters are used to find mid-level managerial talent while retained recruiters focus on the more-senior level leadership positions. In my many years in the workforce, I have been recruited by both, and I have used both. I am not addressing the job placement agencies in this discussion.

Hiring recruiters

If you are embarking on a campaign to find talent outside your organization, I would encourage you to take the time to interview *in-person* those potential firms to ensure alignment with your expectations. As you launch your effort, network, and ask for referrals. Spending the time upfront will almost assuredly save potentially devastating consequences down the road. Just like you would interview more than one general contractor to help you build your new house, take the time to plan your recruitment strategy. And, do not do this in a vacuum. If possible, have your team part of the solution.

As a candidate

Invariably, one day you will get a call from a recruiter. She has a great opportunity. You send your resume. You have the initial phone screen. Everything seems like this could be a very good career move. Mentally, you have already moved on to the new position, and you are dreaming about what the additional compensation means for your future!

HALT!!!!!

Again, I encourage you to ask some questions early in the process. From personal experience, I feel there are a few 'must-asks' before you even send your resume.

Questions to ask

1. Are you retained or contingent? Contingent recruiters tend to flood the hiring manager with resumes, while retained recruiters usually provide a shorter list of more-qualified candidates.
2. How long have you known the hiring manager?
3. What is your track record with that person?
4. Have you been to the hiring company and understand its culture?
5. Have you placed other candidates there? If so, how have they done?
6. Will we be meeting in person before I move on to meet with the hiring company?

Why are these important?

They will set the stage for building a relationship of trust, but perhaps more importantly, they will help you mitigate risk of making a huge career mistake for jumping into a new situation that hasn't been strongly vetted.

Bruce's Thought Box

Leveraging Steve's discussion about reliability and trusted agents, let's look at some of the other traits trusted agents tend to exhibit.

Provide Unfiltered Feedback

One of the benefits of a trusting relationship is that those involved feel comfortable providing candid and direct feedback.

In working with executives one of the things I watch for is a critical observer, that person who will provide honest feedback and protect against groupthink. If an executive asks about this, I usually respond, paraphrasing William Wrigley Jr., 'When two people in an organization always agree one of them is unnecessary.'

Like critical observers, our trusted agents can tell it like it is providing great unfiltered feedback that will broaden our perspective and possibly help us avoid mistakes that could sabotage our legacy. If we are surrounded by people who provide nothing but positive feedback and agreement we miss out on valuable inputs that could make the journey less difficult.

Have Pure Intent

It is important to note that we value and accept input from our trusted agents because they have earned the right. Their actions and clear support for our efforts makes it acceptable to receive critical observations from them.

We know they have our best interest at heart. Without concern about their motives, posturing, or sabotage we simply accept their feedback and assistance. Again, they have earned this right.

Have Your Back

Both Steve and I have a circle of friends ranging from high school and college team mates to people we have served with that we trust implicitly. It is common when someone is struggling or navigating life's challenges for us to rally around and make sure things turn out well. There is no more calming phrase than 'I got your six" when the going gets tough.

Knowing someone is always in your corner and interested in your success makes the journey to achieving your legacy a bit easier. What's the old phase? Many hands make light work.

In thirty years of helping individuals, teams, and organizations, I can say with great confidence that the probability of success is greatly enhanced when there are others on the journey with you who are bought into your vision or purpose and willing to 'take fire' when you are under assault.

Safe Disagreement

The next trait is probably the most relevant for our world today considering the level and type of discourse that takes place. I recently latched onto a phrase I adore, courtesy of Greg Gutfeld on The Five.

"Just because we disagree, it does not mean that I find you disagreeable."

My friends (trusted agents) create a safe place for discussion and disagreement. In person or on social media we give each other great deference. In fact, when there are trusting relationships people tend to be more open to alternative thoughts and giving them a fair hearing. Thoughts, questions, and disagreements are considered when a trusted agent is the source. I am embarrassed to admit that the same statement coming from someone who has lost or abused my trust would not get the same treatment.

You see, my friends come from different backgrounds, walks of life, and political persuasions. If we take offense or hold a grudge our beautiful friendships might be tested beyond repair. For me that would be a tragedy. I believe they feel the same.

As you pursue your legacy it makes sense to have others traveling with you who are reliable, provide valuable feedback, support your success for all of the right reasons, bring talents to bear where you might be less inclined, and can agree to disagree.

Do you have a circle of trust established to support your legacy?

Bruce's Perspective-Pitfalls or Landmines

When trust is present and you have a well-developed circle of trusted agents around you it is both evident and wonderful. Unfortunately, there are times when this is not the case. Let's look at a few examples of what gets in the way of a solid, trusting relationship.

Too trusting of others

Steve and I have often discussed how long it takes to establish a trusting relationship. As you might guess, in order to fulfill Steve's need for reliability, some time may need to pass to prove someone is reliable.

My perspective is a bit more flexible. I believe some of us have the ability to 'thin slice' as presented in Malcolm Gladwell's best seller *Blink* using limited data to make important decisions including if trust is warranted.

Where Steve and I do agree is that if you are too trusting of others without foundation, a positive outcome is questionable at best.

Failing to gain trust or establish a framework for trust

This is the flip side of the same coin. Expecting others to trust us without earning that trust is also fraught with peril. As was the case with Steve's engineer, if a foundation for trust is not in place any misstep can erode trust to a point that may be unrecoverable. If trust is a requisite for building your legacy, it warrants the time and effort to provide proof of your trustworthiness.

Thinking you are more approachable than you are

Many of the executives I have worked with over the years have had a consistent surprise in their organization climate surveys or 360^0 surveys. Regardless of gender, background, education, or industry they were surprised to find out their employees were hesitant to discuss bad news with the executive. The data typically showed employees were fearful of providing bad news because they thought the executive would not respond well. To a person the executives thought they were much more approachable than those who worked with and for them believed. The executives well-honed confidence, decisiveness, and get-to-point approach left those around them with the impression that they were not accessible.

If it takes time and actions to establish trust, thinking you are approachable when others do not, makes a trusting relationship more difficult. Open door policies and encouragement to speak up are nice but not sufficient. Some of your biggest strengths may need to be governed while you prove you are trustworthy.

Assuming you have consensus

Like approachability, consensus can be tricky. Some leaders take silence as acceptance. If someone questions your approachability and openness to a dissenting opinion it is unlikely they will let you know that consensus has not been reached. It is hard to achieve success when you are not sure if everyone is on board. When others react differently than you assumed they would trust will be a casualty.

Steve's Thought Box

How do you establish trusting relationships?

Be observant

How do others communicate with you? In person? Text? Email? Phone? I have found the most-enduring work relationships ALWAYS have the direct, human component to them. How often have you sent an email to someone then walked right past the person's office without saying a word?

Check for assumptions

Seek input from those who have earned your trust. Just like keeping weeds out of the garden, trust must be nurtured and measured. Check in with your agents. Have the difficult conversations. Make adjustments.

Check to ensure true agreement/consensus

Don't you think it is ironic that truth and trust both start with the same three letters? Being honest to one self and honest to others is fundamental to establishing lasting trust. When establishing a lasting foundation for trust, be truthful. Understand your weak points and work to overcome them, if possible. Get feedback from others. Gain consensus to ensure understanding on your legacy. After all, it is your legacy, and you are the only person who can control that.

Bruce's Thought Box

How do you establish trusting relationships?

Trust Equation: Give Trust to Get Trust

My first exposure to this concept was an internal Franklin Covey sales meeting presentation by Dr. Stephen Covey, the author of the all-time business best seller *The 7 Habits of Highly Effective People*. He noted that you cannot Synergize (Habit 6) if you do not give trust to get trust. According to Dr. Covey, the 'give trust to get trust' paradigm is the foundation for Think Win-Win (Habit 4) and Seek First to Understand, Then be Understood (Habit 5).

The concept is actually quite simple in its design and equally powerful in its impact. For many the first trusting relationship began shortly after birth, when you really didn't have much choice. You had to trust those big people with the constant goofy grin for everything from nourishment to personal hygiene. In the years that followed you and your parent(s) exchanged trust. They trusted that you would try to walk and you trusted that they would not let you fall. You trusted they were serious about the rules and earned their trust, with some rare exceptions, by being trustworthy. They extended trust to your friends and soulmate and these extended family members trusted them in return.

I won't belabor the point, we have all had experiences where a goal or objective was not achieved because trust was missing in key relationships required for success. Most of us have also been on teams where we trusted each other implicitly and accomplished great things.

If trust is a requisite for a successful legacy, it probably makes sense to hedge your bet and extend trust to gain trust and accelerate the process.

What impact might the acceleration of the trust process have on your legacy?

Chapter Five

Element 5

Uniquely Designed to Be and Do

"Your life has been intentionally designed by God to have a uniquely significant and eternal impact on the world around you."

Tony Dungy

The Voice Competitors

There are examples all around us of individuals who are doing what they clearly were meant to do. We are also surrounded by those who are clearly off path. The latter are typically struggling to make their life work and very unhappy. On the other hand, individuals who appear to be on purpose attack life and for the most part are almost euphoric doing that thing they were uniquely designed to do.

I grew up in a household where music was a constant. My dad and older brother, Ed, played the trumpet and both earned money during college doing so. Dad had a reel-to-reel player during my teen years and created what I would call the precursor to mixed tapes. Our lives were filled with Motown, Jazz, Big Band, R&B, and Country music. The point being that my childhood set the stage to be an avid viewer of shows like The Voice. The wonderful, eclectic music aside what I am truly drawn to are the singers themselves.

The older competitors normally have made some life sacrifice due to illness of a family member, loss of a parent, being thrust into parenthood at a young age, or navigating life's hard knocks. A little voice calling them back to music is often present. In most cases they have pushed this calling into the background to serve others. The younger competitors, in contrast, are getting an opportunity to determine if singing professionally is what they were meant to do and be. Both old and young are seeking validation of their beliefs that they were uniquely designed to sing.

Watching the process is fascinating. Each singer carrying a belief in their design and a doubt about their ability to prove to others that they 'belong,' take the stage.

The initial selection of the season's competitors is done in the blind. That is to say, the judges have their backs to the competitors so the coaches can only judge the competitors on their voice (singing). In this initial phase putting on a show or how one looks is irrelevant.

Almost to a person the singers take the stage and begin with some trepidation. Each singer drifts into their song and quickly tries to find their footing. As they drift into this place where they feel most at home the singing takes over and the fear and stress begin to dissipate. When the first judge votes by turning their chair around, meaning the singer will be participating in this season's competition, the performer blossoms before our eyes. The singers move to full throat and it becomes clear in an instant that they are doing what they were designed to do.

Age, race, gender, and background are irrelevant. The singers are joyful, emotional, and have arrived at a moment where there is absolute clarity about their design and that they are now on purpose. Naturally, there is only one winner. It is reality TV after all. However, their lives are changed forever. That little voice calling them to sing has been validated.

You see, when we are doing what we are uniquely designed to do we know it. Our heart, mind, and body are totally engaged. Upon reflection it brings out emotions we have not felt in years or in some cases ever.

So, what can we learn from The Voice competitors?

Lessons Learned

- Because of our unique design there is a place in the world where we fill most at home.

- Some people discover their uniqueness and purpose at a young age.

- There are those who put their dreams on hold along with their talents but it is never too late to pursue what you are uniquely designed to do.

- There are some people who have no clue where they are going, what their purpose is, and the talents they bring to the table.

Let's explore each of these lessons in a bit more detail.

At Home

My earliest memory of the phase 'at home' occurred around age 7 or 8 years old. If memory serves, we had been notified that we were reassigned and heading to Germany. During the eighteen months we had lived in Texas we added a furry family member named Kris. Kris was young puppy when he came into our lives. He was a beautiful border collie and the perfect dog for young, energetic boys. He was an indoor dog and we represented the only world he had ever known.

Because of the rules for transporting a dog to Germany at that time Mom and Dad let us know we would have to leave Kris behind. They let us know that a cattle rancher had responded to the newspaper ad and that we would be taking Kris out to the ranch that weekend.

When we arrived at the ranch Kris slowly exited our station wagon and shyly greeted the rancher. After some pleasantries the rancher suggested that we introduce Kris to the cattle. As soon as the rancher opened the gate Kris was off and began herding the cattle. He was running, barking, circling and guiding. It was amazing. Although my hopes that it wouldn't work out and we would keep him were dashed, it was incredible watching him use his innate abilities.

We visited the rancher one last time before leaving for Germany and I will always remember him saying Kris was **at home** on the ranch. I fully understood what that meant when Kris greeted us at the gate and then ran off to do what he was meant to do.

As you craft your legacy, it is our hope that you find a place where you are most 'at home.' Kris surely learned what humans mean by 'do what you love and you won't work a day in your life.'

Early Awareness and Success

We have already broached this subject a couple of times (i.e., six-year old priest, young chef, and young pilots) so we won't spend an unwarranted amount of time in this chapter.

You know the punch line: We are often aware of our unique design at a young age.

Some people are lucky enough to get on path shortly after an innate talent emerges. There are countless stories of young men and women who showed talent well beyond their years. They represent all walks of life.

Here are some examples:

- Athletes (Christian Pulisic, Lebron James, Wayne Gretzky)
- Scientist (Stephen Hawkins, Da Vinci, Madame Curry)
- Entrepreneurs (Steve Jobs, Mark Zuckerberg, Phil Knight)
- Singers (Charlotte Church, Michael Jackson, Elvis)
- Actors (Quvenzhane Wallis, Jackie Cooper, Anna Paquin)
- Politicians (JFK, Theodore Roosevelt, Queen Elizabeth II)

While I have chosen to focus on mostly historic figures here, I have no doubt there are many young people reading this book who are on path, know their talents, and using their unique design to accomplish great things.

Never too Late

Accolades go to those who discover their purpose and talents at a young age. And, equal credit goes to those who find their way at a later point in their lives. While life and delays happen, it is important to note that it is never too late for you pursue what you are uniquely designed to do or be.

Here is a case in point.

Several years ago, *Entrepreneur* magazine published an article entitled *10 People Who Accomplished Great Success After Turning 60.* The article provides a wonderful sampling of individuals who graphically display it is never too late.

Here are of few of the individuals the *Entrepreneur* article highlighted:

Frank McCourt
Literature

Became a bestselling author at 66. Won the Pulitzer Prize for *Angela's Ashes* and sold over 5 million copies.

Laura Ingalls Wilder
Literature

Began writing 'Little House' books at 65. Wilder won several awards and the books were immortalized in the popular *Little House on the Prairie* TV series.

Estelle Getty
Acting

Achieved widespread fame on *The Golden Girls* at 63. The show ran for seven years.

Grandma Moses
Art

Became a folk-artist and cultural icon at 78. After her paintings were discovered in a drugstore window they were exhibited at the MoMA in New York. The pictures appeared on greetings cards, posters and china plates.

Colonel Harland Sanders
Business

Established the Kentucky Fried Chicken restaurant chain at 65. Nine years and 600 franchises later, the Colonel sold his share of KFC for $2 million dollars.

I am in awe every time I think about these 'find your stride late in life' examples.

Obscure Legacy

The final lesson from The Voice performers involves those who are unclear about their purpose, gifts, and potential legacy. I hear this more often than you might expect and a case could be made that this book is written for people who lack clarity of purpose.

As the second largest generation (1945-1965) leaves the workforce in great numbers many are searching for what comes next. This generation does not look like their parents at age 65 or older. The members of this group benefited from knowledge about healthy foods and the dangers of tobacco, being more active, and modern medicine. They are living longer and have more time to impact the world post-career.

During workshops with these Boomers, as they are sometimes called, it appears time and focus are the prime reasons for lack of clarity about their legacy. Many have been so focused on their careers and work deliverables they just didn't carve the time to think about what ideally comes next.

Additionally, when individuals managed to carve the time to think about the next chapter they lacked a focused approach to do so. Blind spots in personal traits and core principles hampered efforts to define a legacy. As we have described herein, focus can be achieved by putting the legacy in perspective, identifying core values, clarifying purpose, engaging trusted agents, and getting clear on innate talents. These are the elements of the legacy blueprint we advocate.

For those seeking assistance defining unique design we offer two approaches for gathering anecdotal information in support of your efforts.

Past Performance as a Predictor

It is a long-held principle of behavioral interviewing that the best predictor of future performance is past performance. Using this as a foundation it follows that one way to gain clarity about a person's innate talents is to look at what talents surfaced in the past. A kind of case-based reasoning for uncovering your native talents.

What does your past tell you about your unique design?

Here are some questions that might help you identify your intrinsic talents:

Where have you had success in the past and what skills/talents were used?

When you were recognized for outstanding contribution (school, work, community) what talents did you display?

What talents seem to surface without much effort?

When you are at the top of your game what skills are you employing?

How are you behaving and what talents are being used when you feel 'at home?'

Most likely the answers to some or all of these questions provides insight into your unique design. While we may have talents that we don't necessarily like to employ, for the most part when we are doing or being what we are intended to do we know and feel it.

Another's Perspective

Another great source for defining your unique design is to seek the inputs of others who know you well. I recommend this based on 30 years of presentations coaching. When left to their own designs human beings will always focus on their faults and downplay their talents. Feedback from others almost always surfaces unacknowledged or hidden talents.

How might others describe your talents/unique design?

There is one sure fire way to find out. Ask!

Go ahead, be transparent and leverage your trusted agents. Let your closest allies know you are working on your next stage of life and would love their input on what you do well and where you might have an impact. Then capture the feedback you receive. No doubt those close to you have thought about the things you bring to the relationship. Your trusted agents have probably wondered why you haven't engaged this career or that activity, because you would be so good at it.

As you probably picked up earlier in the book, I am not a big fan of unsolicited feedback. Consequently, I hold back what could be valuable feedback until I am asked. If someone is very important to me and I feel they are being very tough and unfair to themselves I might ask permission to share my perspective. It is always much easier to share when they ask.

One last thing here. If you ask for feedback please receive it with grace and assume good intent. It is okay not to take action on the feedback or to use it in a different way. It is not okay to be defensive, debate the feedback without a fair hearing, or discount a compliment.

Steve's Perspective--Pitfalls or Landmines

What are some of the barriers to linking your unique design to your dream/legacy?

I believe it really starts with you understanding you. And honestly, it took me about 65 years for me to truly understand me. For a variety of reasons, I obfuscated the real Steve believing it would be better to be someone else other than the real me. Well, I finally figured it out...or nearly have done so. I would encourage you to really dig into who you are now, believe me it won't change, but what might change is your understanding of you. Have others help. Perhaps, there are professional resources, such as counseling, which might prove valuable.

Begin by developing your persona and profile. Refine that. Ask for feedback. Get it right, for what you 'become' will help you focus on your legacy.

Steve's Thought Box

How can you do to define your unique design?

1. Ask your trusted agents to identify your core values, your strengths, and your areas for improvements.

2. Measure those inputs against those you have self-identified.

3. Put a plan in place to continuously improve to some future state only you can define.

4. Measure your successes and failures. Plan for mid-course corrections, and don't waiver from getting to the end state.

Chapter Six

Taking Inventory

"At the center of your being you have the answer; you know who you are and you know what you want."

Lao Tzu

The Five Elements of a Lasting, Personal Legacy

One of the reasons I jumped at the opportunity to work with Steve on this book is a firm belief that C-Level Officers think differently.

Proof came in the form of a conversation during one of our planning calls. I was describing my thoughts on the book and its content. Steve let me go on for a bit interjecting 'fine,' 'I see,' and an occasional 'Uh Huh.'

When I finished my high-energy diatribe, Steve did what great senior executives tend to do. He reinforced the concepts he supported, edited or added to the ideas he didn't, and then stated his greatest concern.

"What I hope to avoid is just writing a book that expresses our thoughts about Legacy but doesn't provide actionable advice."

Steve continued:

"Let's ensure we provide a practical way for others to explore, create, and implement their legacy."

Taking his request to heart this chapter was born. We have already provided the foundation for a *Legacy Play*. You know that the key elements are putting the legacy in perspective, identifying your core values, being clear on your purpose, building trust and engaging trusted agents, and knowing what you were uniquely designed to do and be.

So, the key question is: ***How do you define your best self?***

The remainder of this chapter is dedicated to simple tools for examining each of the key elements listed above. Beginning with your core Values.

Values and Non-Negotiables

We have established how values impact the success of your legacy. If you have not worked on/selected your top values in the past, we have provided a simple process you can use to determine your core values. Additionally, if it has been some time since you defined your core values it might be worth a revisit.

Values Identification Exercise

Steps

1. Using Post-It Notes or index cards make one value card for each of the values on the following pages.

2. Read through the deck of cards one time to get an idea of all the values available.

3. Sort the values into to three piles: Extremely Important to Me, Important to Me, and Not Important to Me.

4. When you have all of the values cards in a pile, pick up the pile designated Extremely Important to Me and select your top five.

   a. If you are struggling getting down to five values start by looking to see if there are overlapping values, that is, do two values accomplish the same end? For example, Achievement and Fame, or Socially Responsible, Contribution, and Compassion. Select the one that best represents your core values.

   b. Do paired comparisons with the remaining cards selecting the top card in each pairing until to get to your top five.

5. If you wish to prioritize your top five once again use paired comparison to determine the rank order from 1 to 5.

6. Capture your top five on your tablet or a piece a paper for future use.

Values

ACHIEVEMENT to accomplish great success

ADVENTURE to experience exciting things and places

AUTHENTICITY to takes actions consistent with who you are

AUTHORITY to lead and be responsible for others

AUTONOMY to be independent and self-governed

CHALLENGE to engage difficult tasks

COMFORT to have a relaxing and secure lifestyle

COMMITMENT to honor and keep your promises

COMPASSION to empathize and care for others

CONTRIBUTION to give assistance or support to a cause

COOPERATION to work well with others

CREATIVITY to generate ideas with your imagination

DILIGENCE to work hard on a task

FAME to be well known and recognized for your accomplishments

FAMILY to have a loving, healthy family

FRIENDSHIP to have a deep, supportive relationship with others

GENEROSITY to willingly give things of value to others

GROWTH to expand your knowledge, skill set, or empathy

HEALTH to be physically fit and well

HELPFULNESS to be helpful to others

HUMILITY to be humble and modest

LEISURE having time to rest and enjoy

LOYALTY to be reliable and dependable in support of others

PASSION to have deep feeling about ideas, activities, or people

PURPOSE to have a reason for why you exist and what you do

SELF-ESTEEM to believe and feel good about yourself

SOCIAL RESPONSIBILITY to act to the benefit society at large

SPIRITUALITY to grow and nurture your human spirit or soul

STABILITY to have a life that is consistent and reliable

WEALTH to have an abundance of valuable possessions

WISDOM to acquire insights and knowledge

Exhilarating Purpose

In the purpose chapter we looked at the proof statements for determining you are on purpose/path and find that vision exhilarating. Here is an approach to clarifying your purpose, ensuring a values match, and validating the proof statements for your purpose.

Exhilarating Purpose Mapping

(2)
Purpose
Why are you doing this?

What does it look like?

_____
_____ **(3)**
_____
_____

(4) **Who will benefit?**

_____
_____
_____
_____

(5)

Values

❑ _____
❑ _____
❑ _____
❑ _____
❑ _____

(6)

Proof Statements

❑ Makes me spring out of bed?
❑ I want to tell anyone who will listen?
❑ Worth fighting through the difficult times?
❑ Makes me fully leverage my best self?

Instructions

Step 1: Draw the diagram (previous page) on your tablet or a piece of paper.

Step 2: At the top of the diagram find the Purpose box and answer the question: Why are you doing this?

Step 3: In the section directly below the Purpose box answer the question: What does it look like?

Step 4: In the next section answer the question: Who will benefit from your pursuit of this purpose?

Step 5: In the section to the left write down your top five core values (identified in prior section). Read your Why, What, and Who and check off the values that are addressed by your Purpose.

Step 6: With your who, what, why, and values in mind place a checkmark next to any and all proof statements that apply in the Proof Statements section.

How do you feel about your Exhilarating Purpose?

What adjustments might you make based on the mapping exercise?

Trust and Trusted Agents

Most legacies involve other people. We typically leave our legacy for others. We sometimes have to get things done through others to make the legacy a reality. And, we often rely on others for feedback, guidance, and support. At the core of all of this is trust.

Trust Audit

One way to evaluate trust in a relationship is to determine whether the traits of trusting relationships discussed in Chapter 4 are present. The audit below provides a way to look at the level of trust.

Word Pairings

☐	Unpredictable	or	Reliable	☐
☐	Hidden Agendas	or	Transparent	☐
☐	Self-Serving	or	Pure Intent	☐
☐	Commit to Anything	or	Make & Keep Promises	☐
☐	I am Always Right	or	Safe Disagreement	☐
☐	Expect Trust	or	Give Trust	☐

Instructions:

Step 1: Select a trust relationship to evaluate.

Step 2: With that relationship in mind, determine which word in each pairing is most descriptive of the person in the relationship. For example, if he/she is more reliable than unpredictable put a check in the box next to Reliable.

Step 3: Once you have one trait in each paring, count up the number of check marks on the right-hand side of the pairings and write that number down.

Step 4: Determine the strength of trust in the relationship using the following scale:

6 Check Marks – Extremely Trusting Relationship

4 or 5 Check Marks – Good level of trust

3 Check Marks – Okay for early in a relationship. Work on the traits marked on the left-hand side for improving trust.

1 or 2 Check Marks – Trust is unlikely at this time. Look at the four or five traits checked on the left-hand side and determine if it is possible and worthwhile to work on those traits. If not, most likely this person will not be a trusted agent moving forward.

One additional thought, it might make sense to have the other person in this trust relationship fill out the audit on you as well. This action could be the beginning of a great alliance.

Unique Design

In the chapter on Unique Design we suggested there are two ways you might gain insights into your natural talents. The two exercises below are provided to zero in on those insights.

Past Performance Predictor

Instructions

Step 1: Write Down a situation or two when you were most successful and almost on autopilot:

Step 2: Select the 8-10 Skills/Talents/Traits you leveraged in the situation(s) above:

X	Column 1	X	Column 2	X	Column 3	X	Column 4
	Analysis		Asking Questions		Articulate		Artistic
	Business Acumen		Adaptability		Brainstorming		Curious
	Communication		Conflict Resolution		Fairness		Enthusiasm
	Critical Thinking		Creativity		Financial Management		Health Oriented
	Decision Making		Future Thinking		Good Listener		Imaginative
	Delegating		Empathy		Initiative		Life Long Learning
	Leadership		High Energy		Inspiring		Networking
	Planning		Inventiveness		Good Listener		Organized
	Problem Solving		Positiveness		Logistics		Outgoing
	Reliability		Persuasive		Marketing		Playful
	Strategic Planning		Self-Assurance		Multi-Lingual		Relationship Oriented
	Systems Management		Story Telling		Negotiating		Wisdom

Step 3: Add up the number of Skills/Talents/Traits selected in each column.

Step 4: Map your results to the Legacy Type they support using the following Key:

Column 1: Career Contribution

Column 2: Community Service

Column 3: Change the World

Column 4: Tending to the Heart

Step 5: Use the results to inform your decisions on the Legacy Type Scoreboard later in this chapter.

Another Perspective Interview

The second approach to identifying the skills/talents/traits that contribute to your unique design is to seek inputs from one of your trusted agents. The Interview below provides a methodology to collect those inputs.

Set up: State something like:

"I recently read a book on creating and leaving a legacy. One of the things the book suggested is to identify skills and talents that are natural for me. Thank you for assisting me by providing your thoughts. I have a few questions."

Question 1: Can you tell me about a challenge or situation you observed where I appeared to use skills or talents naturally with little effort?

Question 2: What were the skills or talents I exhibited?

Question 3: Have you seen me use this skill set in other situations or was it a one off?

Question 4: Are there other situations where you felt I was totally in the zone?

Question 5: What additional skills would you highlight?

Question 6: Knowing me as you do, what would you predict as my next move or legacy?

Again, please use this data to inform your Legacy.

Legacy in Perspective

When all is said and done, the purpose of the work you have completed in this chapter all serves to help put your Legacy in perspective. Using what you have learned from the preceding exercises let's select the type of Legacy you will use as your primary type.

Legacy Type Scorecard

Legacy ➡ Type	Career Contribution	Community Service	Changing the World	Tending to the Heart
Values Match				
Exhilarating Purpose				
Trusted Agents				
Unique Design				
Impact				
Total Scores				

Instructions

Step 1: Beginning with Values Match, determine which Legacy Type best fits with your values. Give the top type a 5. For example, if you think Changing the World is the best fit for your values, give it a '5' ranking.

Step 2: Still ranking your Values Match Rate the remaining Legacy Types using a score of 4 or lower for each.

Step 3: Repeat this process for each Trait (Exhilarating Purpose, Trusted Agents, Unique Design, Impact) until you have filled out the entire scorecard.

Step 4: Add the scores for each column beginning with Career Contribution. The Legacy Type with the highest score is most likely your Legacy Play.

Step 5: Capture your thoughts on why this Legacy Type makes sense.

Some questions to get you started:

- Does it have the potential to have the impact you desire?
- Can you visualize what this legacy might look like?
- Are you excited about this vision?
- What actions will you take immediately to set this legacy in motion?
- Who will you trust to help, support, and give you feedback along the way?

Steve's Thought Box

Falling into a routine can be fatal for your career. Are you being challenged? Do you enjoy your work? Do you leap from bed or drag yourself out only to make every excuse possible to delay your workday start?

Cheerleading

As a manager or senior executive, many eyes are upon you...every day of the week. But, the most important eyes looking at you reflect in your mirror every morning. Can you look at yourself and say you gave it your all? Short of an illness or other serious event which leads to distraction, that is what those who know themselves do every day...be their own cheerleader. Remember, enthusiasm is contagious. Whether it is work, play, or a relationship, give it your all.

Mentorship

If you are a leader (note, I have not said manager), one of the greatest legacies you could potentially impart is that of being a mentor. Some companies have rudimentary mentor programs, but my experience is most fail miserably. That means you, as a leader, or future leader, must take up the slack and fill that void. Like being a good parent who treats her children consistently and fairly, you, as a leader OWE it to be a good mentor. Obviously, one cannot be a mentor to everyone, so you will have to choose. Recognizing future potential makes mentorship application easier. And, mentorship isn't telling someone how or what to do...it is an art of suggestion getting the mentee to think about HOW to respond to a particular set of inputs. Your job is to be there if and when they fall so you can say, "Guess what? I goofed too..."

Then, you can show your vulnerability. Humility is a hallmark of a great leader. Don't be reluctant to show and highlight your failures and vulnerability. You will gain immediate trust with those around you.

In conclusion, do you show your team, regardless if that is your family, your work group, your Thursday night basketball group, etc. you're not perfect? If you do, your stock value will go way up in a hurry.

Chapter Seven

Impact

"The only limit to your impact is your imagination and commitment."

Tony Robbins

Legacy Force

The concept of one's legacy has been on my mind for a long time. Since 2008 the media has stated over and over again that 10,000 Boomers retire each day. While this number is based on when Boomers hit 65 years old and many are working beyond that date, it often gave me pause.

This prompted me to think about what I refer to as the Legacy Force. Imagine what the 65 Million Boomers living today could accomplish if they set out to do good in organizations, communities, and the world. I created a workshop entitled *Boomer Contributions: The Next Chapter* with the pure intent of helping other Boomers create and implement their legacies. I must admit that prior to my conversation with Steve this was the title of the book in my mind and as I have come to believe limited thinking.

As Steve and I explored the generations we were struck by the similarities between the two largest generations: Both of these generations were known as optimistic, convinced they would change the world, questioned authority, and their entrepreneurs and mavericks accomplished great things without finishing college.

This excited me. The Legacy Force grew to a potential of 148 Million (65 m Boomers + 83 m Millennials). Imagine the children, vets, hungry, elderly, homeless, and displaced we could impact in a positive way. Imagine the impact of making your dream come true, whatever it is.

Truly a force for good, a Legacy Force.

What Does Success Looks Like?

"However difficult life may seem, there is always something you can do and succeed at."

Stephen Hawking

The great thing about legacies is that we get to define and create our own vision of success. The preceding chapter, Chapter Six, is intended to provide some insights and assistance in this regard. The 'Why' in your Exhilarating Purpose Mapping provides insight into what success looks like.

Two things come to mind in defining success.

First, having a clear picture of **who does what by when and who it benefits** is a requisite for leaving a successful legacy. Defining what success looks like should be done early in the process of defining your legacy. It will serve as your true north and should make you want to spring out of bed and navigate the tough times.

Second, ownership is key. When we own our legacy, it takes on a different level of import. Think of how you treated a rented apartment or dorm room in contrast with how you treat a home you own. How differently do you treat a rental car than one you own? Create your dream, make it your own, and watch as you move heaven and earth to make it come true.

Spending ample time on developing your picture of success is an imperative and well worth the effort. Let's look at what success might look like for the different legacy types.

Societal Impact (Community Service and Change the World)

For those drawn to having a positive impact on society there is an abundance of opportunities to contribute. I have chosen to combine Community Service and Change the World Legacy Types here because the values, purpose, and skill set are very similar. Let's explore these legacy types a bit more closely using values, talents/traits, and some examples.

Typical Values

Commitment, Compassion, Cooperation, Diligence, Generosity, Helpfulness, Passion, Purpose, Social Responsibility

Typical Skills/Talents/Traits

Asking Questions, Adaptability, Articulate, Brainstorming, Conflict Resolution, Creativity, Empathy, Energetic, Financial Management, Future Thinking, Good Listener, Initiative, Inspiring, Inventiveness, Logistics, Marketing, Multi-Lingual, Negotiating, Persuasive, Positiveness, Self-Assurance, Story Telling

Examples of Societal Impact

The 'Who' providing the impact here includes individual activist, individuals serving as a small non-profit organization, those working with a local or state government organization, or working with a worldwide organization.

Examples of Societal Impact:

What	Beneficiaries
Feed the Hungry	Children, Families, The Poor, the Elderly, and the Homeless
Homes for those in Need	Working Poor, Homeless Vets, Addicts and the Mentally Ill
Elder and End of Life Services	The Elderly and the Terminally Ill
Voter Registration	Voters and the Local Community
HOA Board Member	Neighbors and the Community
Stable Home and Family	Foster Children, Orphans, Latchkey Children
Literacy for All	Adults, Dropouts, Prisoners, those with an Intellectual Disability
Protecting Animals Who Can't Protect Themselves	Abused pets, Animals Used for Gambling, Endangered Species, Animals Killed for Ivory

Strong Enterprises, innovations, and Job Creation (Career Contribution)

Individuals with a legacy focused on career contribution usually contribute in three ways: continued work for a corporation, becoming a small business owner, or self-employment as an independent consultant. Once again let's take a deeper dive.

Typical Values

Achievement, Authority, Challenge, Commitment, Cooperation, Diligence, Fame, Growth, Loyalty, Stability, Wealth, Wisdom

Typical Skills/Talents/Traits

Analysis, Business Acumen, Communication, Critical Thinking, Decision Making, Delegating, Leadership, Planning, Problem Solving, Reliability, Strategic Planning, Systems Management

Examples of Career Contributions

The 'Who' providing the impact here includes Corporate Executives, Small Business Owners, Entrepreneurs, Inventors, and Independent Consultants.

Examples of Corporate Contribution

What	Beneficiaries
Create New Technologies	Schools, Other Businesses, End Users, Other Technologist, Society at Large
Develop and Test New Drugs and Medical Protocols	Patients, Doctors, and Corporations
Job Creation	Employees and their Families, Communities, Local and online Businesses where employees spend their paychecks
Community Support	Charities, People in Need, Cities, Communities, Towns and Youth Leagues
Mentoring the Next Generation of Corporate Leaders	New Leaders, the Associates they will lead, Corporations, Clients and Customers
The Nation's Financial Well-Being	Corporations, Start-Ups, Government Programs, Small Business Owners, and Retirees

Relationships, Hobbies, Unfulfilled Dreams
(Tending to the Heart)

This category in many cases could be labeled 'unfinished business.' Those who choose this legacy type tend to be making up for lost time with families, friends, neglected talents, and delayed adventures. While at first blush this legacy type may seem to be a bit ego-centric, reconnecting with family, friends, talents, and adventure almost always impacts others today and far into the future.

Typical Values

Adventure, Authenticity, Autonomy, Challenge, Comfort, Creativity, Family, Friendship, Growth, Health, Leisure, Passion, Spirituality

Skills/Talents/Traits

Artistic, Curious, Enthusiasm, Health Oriented, Imaginative, Life-Long Learner, Networking, Organized, Outgoing, Playful, Relationship Oriented, Wisdom

Examples of Tending to the Heart

What	Beneficiaries
Seeing the World	Fellow Travelers, Tour Guides, Hospitality Staff, Shop Owners, Those that Experience the Adventure vicariously
Reconnecting with Family or setting an example for Children/Grandchildren	Family and Extended Family.
Acting in a Play or Musical	Fellow Actors, Audience, those impacted by a display of courage, Those embolden to follow your lead.
Athletic Competition	Fellow Athletes, Fans, Coaches and Trainers, and Future Athletes motivated by your strength and courage
Playing an Instrument	Fellow musicians, Audience, Family, Friends, Young Musicians inspired by your performance

Best-Laid Plans

"The best-laid plans of mice and men often go awry."

Robert Burns

I would be remiss if I discussed the impact of your legacy without acknowledging that sometimes things don't go as planned. As is the case with most things in life changes, challenges, and course corrections occur. Everything from health to finances can waylay your legacy. Given the likelihood that 'life will happen' it makes sense to think about contingencies as you build your Legacy Play.

Ask questions to explore potential roadblocks:

What might get in the way?

What resources are necessary for success?

Are the necessary resources in place?

How do I handle changes to my original plan?

What challenges might I encounter?

Use the answers to these and other questions to create contingency plans and increase your agility in responding to potential challenges.

As you implement your legacy do a status check periodically by asking:

What is working?

What is helpful but not working yet?

What is not working?

In response make small course corrections leveraging what is working, improving things that are beneficial but not fully baked, and discarding things that are not of value.

Steve's Perspective-Pitfalls and Landmines

What might go wrong?

Apathy. Each of us is pulled in so many directions. How does one overcome apathy?

Just like putting money in the bank (does anyone do that anymore?), MAKE TIME for yourself. I recall my dad telling me what his dad (my paternal grandfather) used to do. He would wake up in the middle of the night with an idea. Nothing unique about that. But, he kept a pad of paper and a pencil on the nightstand. He would jot down words and/or a drawing so that he had permanent record of an idea that came to him during the night. He was ready. That protocol led to my grandfather applying for two patents relating to tool designs. He found a way to make time for himself.

What's the point? Don't get into a rut. Find a way to stay mentally in the game.

Loss of personal vision

Obviously, I don't mean eyesight. How many of us have been asked to author or help in the development of a strategic plan? But, have you asked yourself to develop your own plan? Do you network? Do you keep your resume up to date? Do you have a vision for what and where you want to be in 2, 5, and 10 years? If not, I would encourage you to sketch that out. Ask others who have been down those roads what they did. Have your Human Resources department to accomplish a peer or a 360 review.

You can't get to where you want to be without planning for it. Plans are insignificant, but *planning* is the key.

Steve's Thought Box

What can you do to keep or get your legacy on track?

1. Establish your personal strategic plan with the singular goal of your personal legacy. Just like you would do for any business, establish your personal strengths, weaknesses, opportunities, and threats. Build upon the strengths, work to overcome or obviate the weaknesses, turn the opportunities into reality (strengths), and understand how the threats put at risk all you have built to date.

2. Measure it. Modify it, as necessary. Ask trusted agents for input. Be honest, and most importantly,

3. **Hold yourself accountable**.

Chapter Eight
Cost of Doing Nothing

"Strange, isn't it? Each man's life touches so many other lives. When he isn't around he leaves an awful hole, doesn't he?"

**Clarence Oddbody Character in
'It's a Wonderful Life'**

Questions About Life's Purpose

When one's thoughts about legacy begins is probably as varied and unique as the legacy being created. And, it seems to be a universal truth that most humans at some point question their life's purpose and what they will leave behind when they are gone.

The questions are countless:

"What example have I set for my children and their children?"

"How does this job, career, activity, action make a difference?"

"What good have I done for the world I leave behind?"

"What difference have I made in someone else's life?"

"Nothing seems to change or get better. What impact, if any, have I had?"

"How have I helped someone less fortunate?"

"What is new, better, improved, changed by my actions?"

It is natural for us to question our purpose, influence, impact, and worth. As noted in an earlier chapter, people also seem inclined to diminish or discount their worth when it comes to the legacy they create.

So, we thought it appropriate to beg the question:

What would a world without you look like?

A Life Without You

One of my favorite holiday classics is *It's a Wonderful Life*. The story centers around George Baily a hard-working, charitable man played by Jimmy Stewart. The audience gets to know George and see how life takes its toll.

At a crucial point in the movie George is given an opportunity to see what the world would look like if he had never been born. He is taken on this journey by Clarence Odd Body, an Angel 2nd Class trying to earn his wings (quoted at the beginning of this Chapter). Clarence shows George how his absence impacts his wife, children, his hometown, and his business. Needless-to-say, the voids created by George's absence are many and significant.

As I began putting pen to paper (okay keystroke to screen) I remember being motivated by all the of impact and influence your legacies represent. When writer's block or real world intervened another more significant motivation took hold. It was the despair I felt thinking about a world where you failed to pursue that thing, cause, dream, or vision you were put on this earth to do. The sadness was palpable when I thought about the people who so badly need your example, wisdom, support, grace, love, and passion.

When 'life happens' and your legacy is challenged please take a moment to reflect on the void your absence would create.

What are the costs if you fail to pursue your legacy?

People

Recently I conducted what could be loosely defined as a survey on Facebook. My friends and contacts were asked whether they had a legacy in mind. Almost everyone responded by noting others who would be the beneficiaries. Most referenced their children and grandchildren and the example they tried to set.

Needless-to-say, if we follow the theme of this chapter, countless lives would be impacted if the Facebook respondents did not think about or pursue their legacies. Beyond my friends and contacts, millions of people would feel the absence of a caring benefactor.

Think about the children who would be impacted without coaches, scout masters, volunteers at the YMCA, Big Brothers-Big Sisters, social workers, foster parents, and teachers?

What about those who have lost their way due to drugs, Post Traumatic Stress, or running away from home at a young age? Without the selfless individuals who try to help them find a path back into society, many more would be lost. These same volunteers help at risk youth get their high school and college degrees, so they can find better paying jobs. The adult illiterate would never learn to read if these caring individuals were absent.

Reflect on the millions of employees and their families who would falter if small business owners, entrepreneurs, and corporate leaders failed to think about the lives impacted by their legacies.

Advances in Technology and Medicine

We live in a time of great advancements. Everything from artificial intelligence to unique DNA-related cures for cancer are being researched, designed, created, and discovered.

Living in Silicon Valley, somewhere in a ten-mile radius the next big breakthrough in technology or medicine is being formulated. But, what if that great discovery rests with someone who is neither encouraged or educated to pursue the advancement?

Are the cures for cancer, ALS, Alzheimer's, Muscular Dystrophy, and autism, one legacy away?

Will technical advances improve work? What about prosthetics that closely emulate the hands and feet they are replacing? Think about the impact on vision and hearing. Take the time to wonder about how technology might impact every aspect of our lives.

There are advances we cannot even imagine that will become a reality because of someone in future generations who we nurture, develop, educate, and encourage.

It is unfathomable to me that a lost legacy might result in a major advancement being discarded or delayed. My hope is that you define, craft, and pursue your unique legacy leaving the world better and greater than it was when you arrived.

Changing the World

"To whom much is given, much will be required."

Luke 12:48

There are two indisputable truths in our world. First, those who reside in First World countries have been given much. Second, many great needs exist in our world.

Imagine a world where a solution to the world's water issues existed but no one cared. What if great progress in fighting homelessness, hunger, and polluted oceans and rivers is within reach but we expect others to step up or wait on divine intervention.

What if dedicated doctors and the non-profit organizations they work with decided their work makes so little difference in a world so daunting, that they stopped giving immunizations, health care, and new smiles to beautiful children around the world.

Can you envision the many endangered, poached, and abused animals without concerned humans waging a battle on their behalf? I'm guessing those unnerving commercials requesting donations would have little impact if the plight of these wonderful creatures did not strike a nerve.

Yes, the world needs of individuals, groups, and philanthropists to right wrongs, help the needy, and care for our planet. Are you called to help? How will you turn your abundance into a blessing for the less fortunate among us?

It is only human to wonder what difference your life makes. We all wonder if our legacy has relevance. Having explored what happens when legacies are unfulfilled, I hope you will have no doubt your life matters and others (in all of their forms) are betting on your gift of time, knowledge, hope, belief, experience, and support.

Steve's Perspective--Pitfalls

What faulty thinking do you engage in when you willfully abandon your legacy?

No one cares

Early in the book, I stated the legacy of creating a legacy may be one of the more important things any of us can learn to do.

Why are legacies important?

There are likely hundreds of answers. To be totally open, I care about what most people think about me. When gone, I hope people say I was a patriot, trustworthy, funny (most would say I am corny!!), and had a strong work ethic, among others.

Don't assume no one cares about you and your legacy. As a minimum, those close to you likely do. Have you asked them? If you are a leader in a company, have you asked your peers? Direct reports? Your boss?

Steve's Thought Box

How can you keep your legacy on track and moving forward?

1. Ideate your future by drafting your resume as you would like it to read in 10-20 years. Don't just focus on jobs and your career but include a vision statement. Translate that vision statement into your draft legacy.

2. As morbid as this may sound, write your obituary. Don't reveal it to anyone but ask yourself if it helps to define and refine your legacy.

Chapter Nine
Final Thoughts

Steve's Final Thoughts

What impact could millions of people pursuing their legacies have on others, businesses, societies, and the world?

Each of us gets caught up in the minutia of living our lives. Will we have enough money to pay the bills? My commute is getting longer. My boss is more demanding. I don't see a future where I am. What's my purpose, or perhaps more importantly, What is my legacy?

Personally, I didn't even think about my legacy until 2016. I am not sure what created the thought spark, but it was likely my age and the realization that I have lived a long life, and that sun is setting. The thought of my legacy and what it might be came and went. I asked my children. Then, I wondered if others were thinking the same? I asked some of those close to me if they were thinking about their legacies, and I got no for an answer each time. Why, I thought? Wasn't it important? Am I overstating the importance?

Maybe creating a legacy isn't for everyone. If you don't think it is now, maybe it will surface later. I know that is what I experienced. This book was intended to develop some ideas, foster self-reflection, and, perhaps, start the planning process for you to create a legacy, or how to create the legacy of legacy realization. Both Bruce and I hope there are enough nuggets of wisdom here to help you get started on that journey should you choose.

Bruce's Final Thoughts

As we put the finishing touches on *Legacy Play* an incredible man and journalist published a final letter to his peers and viewers. His name is Charles Krauthammer and he had just been notified he had only weeks to live following a bout with a particularly aggressive form of cancer.

The final paragraph of his letter resonated with me and provides a wonderful capstone for *Legacy Play:*

"I leave this life with no regrets. It was a wonderful life – full and complete with the great loves and great endeavors that make it worth living. I am sad to leave, but I leave with the knowledge that I lived the life that I intended."

Dr. Charles Krauthammer
1950-2018

Dr. Krauthammer thank you for your grace, wit, intellect, and thoughtfulness. Rest in Peace knowing you impacted millions in a positive way and will be remembered for generations for your courage, intellect, class, and journalistic contributions to society.

It is my hope that each one of you gains clarity about your unique purpose, leveraging your given talents, for the benefit of others in your sphere of influence.

May you live a life worth living as you always intended.

Bruce Michael Goeas

About the authors

Bruce and Steve met in 1984 while each was stationed at Vandenberg AFB, California. Both were Command Briefers in the Strategic Air Command. Their bond was immediately apparent, in and of itself, a legacy. That heritage has continued ever since and will endure for years and decades to come.

Bruce Michael Goeas
Author | Founder | Principal
bruce@bgoeasenterprises.com

Bruce grew up as a 'military brat' and notes that when you move around every 18 months you become very comfortable with change and overcoming the fears inherent in new situations. He is the author of *Where Fear Fails*, dedicated to the mitigation of fear that impacts individual, team, and organizational success.

With over 30 years of experience in Change Management, Leadership Development, Organization Development, and Talent Management; Bruce has worked with clients from the Cayman Islands to the Hawaiian Islands and most places in between. His clients have included companies large and small in Aerospace, Healthcare, High Tech, Finance, Hospitality, and Pharmaceuticals.

Bruce is a retired Air Force Lt. Colonel and lives with his wife Chris, and Maddie their black and white cocker spaniel. Bruce and Chris have been married 39 years.

Steve Darr
Father | Author | Senior Leader/Former C-Level Executive
stevedarr@hotmail.com

Steve is a legacy product of John and Angeline Darr (see Larry King's book, *Love Stories of World War II*), his parents. Steve was born an Air Force dependent. It was his parents' love for country and service, in part, which led him to a ten-year stint in the US Air Force. After three years on Minuteman III Missile Crew at F.E. Warren AFB, Wyoming, Steve spent the next seven years in a variety of staff positions. In 1985, he voluntarily separated from the US Air Force to pursue a career outside the military.

Steve has spent nearly 33 years in private industry with large and small companies and has held positions from Marketing Manager to President/CEO. His extensive P&L responsibilities range from $12M to more than $375M, and he has run multi-national, multi-site companies. It was during his various employs that many of the legacy lessons began to take shape. His many mentors, colleagues, customers, vendors, and others, unknowingly, have provided the constructs which form the basis of much of this book.

When not working on his car, Steve vigorously surfs the internet looking for the next vehicle he cannot afford to own.

Dedications

Bruce Michael Goeas

First and foremost, I dedicate this to my wife, Christina. Her support for the past 42 years has been my lifeblood and it has been a joy to create our legacy together.

Second, Mom and Dad! You taught us how to believe in ourselves, to never abandon our values, and to fight for the underdog. We hope we carry on your legacy in a way that would make you proud. Love you both more than words can describe.

Third, my wonderful brothers Ed, Wayne, and Darryl. Ed for his dedication to ensuring our nation has strong leadership and for the legacy represented by his children and grandchildren. Wayne who creates a new legacy with every building he designs and builds. His architecture produces beautiful, lasting legacies. Darryl for his street ministry, attempting to help others learn from his tough journey through life and make different choices.

Steve Darr

I dedicate this book to many including my parents, without whom I would have never been given the nurturing and start in life. Secondly, I want to acknowledge my brother, George, whose enduring encouragement resonates to this day. Thirdly, I wish to honor my three amazing legacies: Cameron, Janessa, and Zachary. Each possesses unique and indomitable spirits. I look up to each. Fourthly, I wish to recognize my uber-talented wife, Brenda, who has supported me through thick and thin and whose personal outlook on life is one many should emulate and has created a lasting legacy for those around her.

And, finally, I dedicate this book to those who have made *meaningful* impacts on my life. Each has been a major contributor, in a covert way, to the contents of this book.

www.ingramcontent.com/pod-product-compliance
Lightning Source LLC
Chambersburg PA
CBHW052324220526
45472CB00001B/268